Afghan Heritage

Celebrating Diversity in My Classroom

By Tamra B. Orr

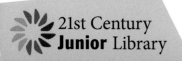

21st Century **Junior** Library

Published in the United States of America by
Cherry Lake Publishing
Ann Arbor, Michigan
www.cherrylakepublishing.com

Reading Adviser: Cecilia Minden, PhD, Literacy expert and children's author

Photo Credits: ©Wandel Guides/Shutterstock, cover; ©Wandel Guides/Shutterstock, 4; ©alexreynolds/
Shutterstock, 6; ©Kent Weakley/Shutterstock, 8; ©luxG4/Thinkstock, 10; ©tiverylucky/Shutterstock, 12;
©Santhosh Varghese/Shutterstock, 14; ©hlphoto/Shutterstock, 16; ©ChiccoDodiFC/Shutterstock, 18;
©Sirisak_baokaew/Shutterstock, 20

Library of Congress Cataloging-in-Publication Data
Name: Orr, Tamra, author.
Title: Afghan heritage / Tamra B. Orr.
Description: Ann Arbor : Cherry Lake Publishing, 2018. | Series: Celebrating diversity in my classroom |
    Includes bibliographical references and index.
Identifiers: LCCN 2018003277 | ISBN 9781534129054 (hardcover) | ISBN 9781534130753 (pdf) |
    ISBN 9781534132252 (pbk.) | ISBN 9781534133952 (hosted ebook)
Subjects: LCSH: Afghanistan—Juvenile literature.
Classification: LCC DS351.5 .O76 2018 | DDC 958.1—dc23
LC record available at https://lccn.loc.gov/2018003277

Cherry Lake Publishing would like to acknowledge the work of the Partnership for 21st Century Skills.
Please visit *www.p21.org* for more information.

Printed in the United States of America
Corporate Graphics

CONTENTS

Kabul is Afghanistan's capital and largest city.

Amazing Afghanistan

Afghanistan is a small country in south-central Asia. It is about the size of Texas. Much of it is covered in snowy mountains and sandy deserts. As of 2017, around 34 million people live in Afghanistan. A small number of Afghans live in the cities of Kabul, Kandahar, and Herat.

For years, millions of Afghans have been forced to leave their country due to war. Most went to nearby Pakistan and Iran. Thousands of others **immigrated** to the United States.

Afghanistan is a mostly-tribal society. Many ethnic groups live there.

Salaam Alaikum!

Listen carefully in Afghanistan. There are many languages spoken there. The country's official languages are Pashto and Dari. Most people in Afghanistan speak one of these as their primary or secondary language.

Dari is mostly used by the government, **media**, and businesses. It comes from the Persian language. Pashto and Dari are very old languages. Both are used in the country's

Pashto is also spoken in Pakistan and Iran.

literature. "Welcome" in Pashto is *"Salaam alaikum!"* In Dari, it is *"As-salamo alaykom!"*

Afghanistan is **landlocked**. It is between South Asia, Central Asia, and Iran. So, many different groups have come through the country. They have shared their languages. Experts believe there are as many as 40 languages spoken throughout Afghanistan.

Many women say their burqa gives them privacy.
It allows them to move freely in public.

One Religion

Almost everyone in Afghanistan is Muslim, followers of Islam. The country's constitution states that other religions are allowed. But it also states that all laws are based on Islamic rules. Many Afghan **traditions** are based on these rules. For example, men and women wear special clothing that covers up their bodies and heads as a show of religious **modesty**.

Afghan hosts often serve grapes and other seasonal fruits to guests.

Men and women do not spend time together if they are not married. Men and women avoid direct eye contact.

Most Afghans welcome visitors into their homes and kindly share tea or a treat. In return, visitors usually bring a small gift to give to their hosts as thanks.

Ask Questions!

Does your family have any religious traditions or customs? Do you pray before meals? Do you go to church services? Do you avoid certain types of food? Ask your parents about any faith-based traditions, when they began, and what they might mean.

Afghans think rice is the best part of a meal.

Kebabs and Sharbat

Afghanistan's national dish was once only served to the very richest families. Today, it is found in many restaurants and homes. *Qabili palau* blends together some very unusual flavors and **textures**. The recipe includes carrots mixed with raisins, slivered almonds, and sugar. Added to that are chicken and properly cooked basmati rice. (Afghan women pride themselves on cooking it *just right*!)

Mantu is served during special events or large gatherings.

Kebabs are long wooden sticks that hold grilled pieces of meat and vegetables. They are commonly served for lunch and dinner.

Rice and onions are the most common ingredients in Afghan dishes. People also enjoy *ashak*, dumplings topped with minced meat and yogurt. *Mantu* are dumplings filled with ground lamb. Afghans drink a great deal of tea, plus *sharbat*, or juice. *Sharbat-e-bomya*, rosewater and lemon juice, is a favorite. So is *sharbat-e-rayhan*, which is rosewater, sugar, and basil seeds.

Some of the most beautiful rugs in the world come from Afghanistan.

An Average Day

Every morning in Afghanistan's large cities thousands of merchants get up, wash, and say their prayers. Then, they throw open their doors and let people know they are ready for business. People push their food carts onto the sidewalks. There are countless honking vehicles, and U.S. soldiers patrol the streets.

In small villages, people begin their day by feeding their cows, sheep, and goats. Children go to school, and their parents start their work. It's another typical day for Afghans.

Men and boys fly kites on Fridays.

For fun, many Afghans fly kites—but not the way most people do. Flying a kite in Afghanistan is an invitation to battle. Kite strings are coated in glue and crushed glass. The hope is that this will slice through another kite's string. Young men climb to the rooftops with their bamboo and tissue paper kites. And the fight is on!

Look!

If Afghans get their way, the Olympic Games of the future will include *buzkashi*, or goat-grabbing. Buzkashi is the country's national sport. Riders on horses try to grab a goat **carcass**. Then they must drop it in just the right place to score a point. It is a violent and fast-paced sport. And women are not allowed to play or watch!

GLOSSARY

carcass (KAR-kuhs) dead body of an animal

immigrated (IM-ih-gray-ted) entered and settled in another country

landlocked (LAND-lahkt) bordered on all sides by other countries and no seas

media (MEE-dee-uh) method of communication between people, such as television, newspapers, and radio

modesty (MAH-dist-ee) reserved in appearance, manner, and speech

textures (TEKS-churz) the ways that something feels, especially how rough or smooth it is

traditions (truh-DISH-uhns) an idea or belief that is handed down

Pashto Words

ashak (ah-SHAHK) dumplings topped with minced meat and yogurt

buzkashi (booz-KAH-shi) goat grabbing

kebabs (kuh-BAHBZ) a common meal of grilled meat and vegetables on long wooden sticks

mantu (MAHN-too) dumplings filled with ground lamb

qabili palau (KAH-buh-li puh-LAUW) Afghanistan's national dish

Salaam alaikum (suh-LAHM ah-LAY-kum) welcome

sharbat (SHAR-buht) juice

sharbat-e-bomya (SHAR-buht-EE-bohm-YUH) rosewater and lemon juice

sharbat-e-rayhan (SHAR-buht-EE-RAY-anh) rosewater, sugar, and basil seeds

Dari Word

As-salamo alaykom (ah-suh-LAH-moh ah-LAY-kohm) welcome

FIND OUT MORE

BOOKS

Glynne, Andy, and Salvador Maldonado. *Ali's Story: A Real-Life Account of His Journey from Afghanistan.* North Mankato, MN: Picture Window Books, Capstone Imprint, 2018.

Hunter, Nick. *Hoping for Peace in Afghanistan.* Oxford: Raintree, 2018.

Mason, Helen. *A Refugee's Journey from Afghanistan.* Ontario: Crabtree Publishing, 2017.

WEBSITES

National Geographic Kids—Afghanistan
www.kids.nationalgeographic.com/explore/countries/
afghanistan/#afghanistan-blue-mosque.jpg
Read about the geography, nature, and history of Afghanistan.

Scholastic—Kids in Afghanistan
www.teacher.scholastic.com/scholasticnews/indepth/afghanistan/
Check out this guide to life in Afghanistan.

The Fact File—66 Interesting Facts about Afghanistan
www.thefactfile.org/afghanistan-facts/
Find out about different aspects of life in Afghanistan.

INDEX

ABOUT THE AUTHOR

Tamra Orr is the author of hundreds of books for readers of all ages. She graduated from Ball State University, but moved with her husband and four children to Oregon in 2001. She is a full-time author, and when she isn't researching and writing books, she writes letters to friends all over the world. Orr enjoys life in the big city of Portland and feels very lucky to be surrounded by so much diversity.